SCUFFED UP

THE STORIES OUR SHOES TELL

SCUFFED UP

How to use your Past Journeys to Overcome your Anxieties and Create a Clear Life Plan.

JILL SHEPHERD

Dedication

This book is dedicated to my incredible husband who has been my biggest supporter for all my crazy ideas and helps me find a way to make them a reality, and my mom who raised me in such a way to discover my own passions and helped me develop a drive to try. I would not have done so much without them.

You have brains in your head.

You have feet in your shoes.

You can steer yourself any direction you choose.

- DR. SEUSS, OH THE PLACES YOU'LL GO

Table of Contents

CHAPTER 1

The Pile of Shoes in Your Closet

"Where so ever you go, go with all your heart."

CONFUCIOUS

It doesn't matter what kind of shoes they are: fancy sandals, trusted tennis shoes, or an old pair of boots you wore through the crazy snow storm last winter. Everyone's shoes are completely different—colors, styles, and shapes—yet they all tell a story.

When you buy a new pair of shoes fresh off the shelf, free of dirt, stains and scuff marks, you are starting a new story. In no time, the shoes become worn, dirty, and scuffed with things you can't erase no matter how hard you try.

After some time, you'll find marks you might actually be proud of! Maybe, there's a green streak on the side of your cleat from that ball-blocking slide that won the soccer game. Or maybe, there's an oil mark on the top from the time you started your first job at a concession stand. There may even be marks you're not so proud of, like the permanent marker

1

on the bottom of your sandals from the cheat sheet you needed for a test. Maybe there's a strap on your favorite heels that is starting to tear from a long business trip you were in charge of.

If someone else looked at your shoes they may only see grass stains, grease, or permanent marker, but when *you* look at them, you remember what made those marks. They're the stories telling of your life.

The stories our shoes could tell. That's why I just love old shoes!

At any given age in my life, you would have probably caught me wearing my beat-up sneakers, except to church. They were and still are my "go-to" shoes. Even if they get old and are barely holding together, I can't seem to let them go. Those "go-to" shoes of yours are, I am sure, hard to get rid of as well because when you look at them, you remember all you did in them.

They reflect your life.

When you reflect on your life, it can take you down many different paths. For me, I was taken back to an old pair of running shoes. They were so old; they had a dusty smell to them. Even the color was no longer white, but a dirty brown from running in the sand when I was stationed in Afghanistan.

I still remember that day; the challenges that emerged just to even get to the starting line. Out of the many races I had done, this was the toughest. As I looked at my shoes years later, I could still recall the painful steps I went through to finish the race. I remembered the doubt that crept in and almost made me quit. Then eventually, empowering thoughts motivated me, helping me re-focus and finish what I started. I never wore those shoes again after that race, but those shoes had a story, a memory, I wanted to relive forever.

By the time I was a sophomore in high school, I liked to get my exercise in at the gym before classes started. I picked up the hobby of running at age sixteen to help add variety to my workouts, but was never a serious runner. I saw this group of adults meet up in the foyer of this gym every morning at 5:30 to run. They looked like they knew what they were doing so, I introduced myself to them and decided to join them on occasion to change up my routine. Any normal sixteen-year-old would want to spend time with people their own age, but I wasn't just any teen. I've often been told I have an old soul because of my mindset and dedication to the things I care about. Little did I know, every single one of them were marathon runners.

I couldn't help but think, *I've surrounded myself with crazy people! Why on Earth would anyone voluntarily run a marathon?*

I thought it was foolish of people to even consider running a marathon. It was like a slow, painful torture. In the amount of time it takes to run 26.2 miles, I could have already went shopping, got my next project for school done, hung out with friends and home just in time for a relaxing bath. I couldn't imagine spending hours running until my feet bled or even hydrating my body enough to stay upright. The cons were endless!

Yet, there was a side of me that was envious of them accomplishing such a feat. Part of me was intrigued by the thought of conquering something as difficult as a marathon.

Could I do it?

The thought ate at me because I knew I could. With a little bit of discipline, which I had a knack for, and a lot of convincing myself the idea of running was actually fun, I knew could do it. The only thing I could think of next was where to start.

It was time for new shoes!

Who doesn't love a new pair of shoes? There's nothing like the feeling of slipping those brand-new shoes on your feet. Whether you're wearing them for an event or for training, every time you put them on your feet, you're gaining the confidence to take the next step.

The first time I bought a pair of Nike™ Air Pegasus running shoes, I felt confident in the decision I had made. Had I gone with my causal, supermarket shoes, which fit the budget more for a high school student, I would have been doctoring my feet every day. The moment I laced them up, I felt confident I could conquer anything. I could picture myself running hard as I crossed over the finish line. The investment in those shoes gave me the courage to embark on a new journey by stepping out of my comfort zone.

In the beginning, I started small, building a pace I would be comfortable enough to withstand long distances. Setting my pace wasn't the only challenge, though. On top of finding the sweet spot to control my breathing, I had the task of overcoming the mental exhaustion of making it through the grueling miles ahead.

Soon I was running eight miles, then ten, and then one day, I finished sixteen miles with the group. I couldn't believe

I ran that far! After finishing, I distinctly remember bending over to rest my hands on my knees, staring at my gently-used running shoes, whispering to them, *"We just did that!"*

Though my breathing was heavy from the amount of energy I exerted, the majority was from the excitement of actually finishing sixteen miles. Everything I had thought was impossible, became achievable the moment I completed my goal. A marathon was only ten more miles, so why couldn't I complete that too?

So, I signed up for my first marathon.

My running conversations now turned from making fun of marathon runners to preparing to be one, and there was nothing like a new pair of shoes to help me begin a new path faster. I discovered new skill sets, ready to empower me, inspiring more confidence in my abilities. That same confidence then gave me the stability I needed to take each grueling step. But most of all, stepping into these new shoes, I wanted to prove to myself I could accomplish anything I set my mind to.

The morning of the race came. Hours before the sun came up, runners of all types bounced on their feet, trying to stay warm. They were ready to create a new story in their shoes, just like me. The confidence I had in my new shoes was quickly fading though. As I looked ahead of me into the darkness, I thought, *Had I done everything I needed?* I ran the distances, I ate the right foods, and I bought the right shoes—yet doubt still crept in. The mental battle had already begun before the physical. I could feel all 26.2 miles mocking me.

It was time to put my game face on.

The starting pistol fired.

Here we go.

I can do this!

Nerves and excitement carried me through the first few miles. By the time I'd hit eleven miles, my feet were starting to hurt. I tried repeating motivational affirmations to myself, but even that was tough since I hadn't even made it halfway yet! Mile by mile, the distance pushed me beyond anything I had ever done in my life. I kept reminding myself the pain would be over in a couple hours, but with each step, the pain spread. My feet felt so bruised I thought they were going to fall off. I wanted to crumble to the ground and not get up for a few hours, but I shook away my tears and pressed forward.

I *wanted* to finish.

I kept moving forward, painful step by painful step, until I saw the finish line. This was it! The moment I knew I would finish. My throat was burning and I was partly crying and hyperventilating while running. Then an overwhelming excitement hit me like a jolt of electricity as the crowd cheered, carrying me to the end. People I had never met before clapped and yelled, "You got this!" Every step felt like my feet were attached to cement, but the overpowering love and encouragement made my heart swell.

The positive energy vibrated through the crowd, and somehow it made me feel lighter. In that moment, the pain seemed to go away, being replaced with a sense of accomplishment. My pace quickened, my heart skipped a beat, and I pushed my tired body across the finish line.

I did it!

Wiping the tears from my face, I stole a glance at my running shoes. My feet were sore, and I couldn't wait to let them breathe outside of the shoes, yet I felt so proud to be wearing them. Without those dirty, scuffed shoes, I wouldn't have made it to this point. I knew exactly what every mark meant, with every challenge I had to overcome. It wasn't about the distance or running for a few hours for exercise. It was about what I taught myself by overcoming such a feat.

I learned that when I hear the doubt and fear in my head; I can shut the negative thoughts down. The pain ached and burned as if my body was scraped up by a hot metal grate, yet I pushed through it. I was empowered with a new skillset to help me in all aspects of life. Though it wasn't easy, and I still had a long journey ahead, I knew I had the strength to do it. I focused my energy on the things I knew gave my life meaning. Through the good, I could overcome the bad.

Rather than saving my skills for a rainy day, I was going to put my rain boots on and jump in the puddles. I promised myself to chase every dream until they became a reality, so I was going to push every limit, discover new skills, and always try on new shoes.

GET OUT OF YOUR COMFORT SHOES

Stepping out of my "go-to" shoes, my comfort zone, made me feel vulnerable. Even though my beat-up sneakers were a secure and safe place for me to be, life is about pushing myself to see how far I can go!

If you just hangout in your comfort shoes, you'll not only miss out on wearing some great styles, but you'll miss out on who you could become. Your life is supposed to be a journey and your shoes can take you to some unique places if you let them. It's up to you to avoid getting stuck in the same place. You don't want to stay too comfortable, always ending up back at the same spot over and over again.

Change is a good thing!

What dreams do you have? What shoes do you imagine strutting around in? What impact do you want to make in those "soles" and on other people?

You might think to yourself, Why do I even need to set goals? I like my life just how it is. I am doing *enough*, and isn't that enough?

I have been guilty of saying this too! I have felt guilty because I believe we are born with this innate desire and drive to continuously grow and improve. After a while of "being comfortable," I found I wasn't happy. I felt like purpose was missing from my life. After completing my first marathon, the excitement I had while training seemed to diminish. I needed to set another goal. I had just graduated high school and was in need of a new adventure.

I knew I could do more.

If you find yourself coasting along in life, like floating down the lazy river in an inner tube, I have some advice for you. Jump off the floatie and swim into the rapids! You only live once, so it's important to make the most of it.

Be motivated by the fear of being average!

Adding adventures to your life, as well as ways to improve who you are, will always add value and meaning to your life. You will find reasons to get up every day. Going after a goal is a lifestyle. Forming and developing habits to architect each day of your life will help you become the person you're meant to be.

Don't just set goals to please others. Do it for *you*. Show *yourself* what you are capable of. You may surprise yourself.

There is a famous saying among runners: "The way you approach a hill is the way you approach life." In my running career, I find it interesting to see what type of runners are around me, it can say a lot about them. When the race kicks off with a bang, runners of all types start the journey, excited and nervous. As it continues, you get to the dreaded hill. Some runners see a hill, and they immediately start to walk; they've already told themselves they don't have a chance. Some see it and get discouraged. Others keep the same pace, thinking slow and steady.

Then there are those, who I strive to be like, who approach it with a "go get 'em" attitude, pushing harder, attacking the hill, unafraid to give it all they've got.

You don't have to be a runner to figure that out about yourself. If anything, we just need to know we, at the very least, don't change pace.

So what type of runner are you?

WHAT ARE YOU AFRAID OF?

I've found that sometimes it's our anxieties holding us back. When I have caught myself coasting along in life to stay safe, I had some retrospection, digging deep as to *why*. I know

I am not alone in these feelings. Some of the most common anxieties keeping us from trying new things and setting bigger goals include:

1. It's too hard
2. Being uncomfortable
3. Doubting your capabilities
4. Fear of the unknown
5. Needing to know everything first
6. Comparison and measuring up
7. Fear of failure
8. Feeling like you are the only one and are embarrassed to ask for help

Throughout this book, you will find ways to help overcome your fears and doubts, change your thought process and perspective, and be armed with the tools to take on any new adventure that comes your way.

Your shoes are waiting for you to get *Scuffed Up*! Your new capabilities hidden inside you are waiting to be discovered and can't be found any other way.

When you put on any pair of shoes, whether it's for school, work, interviews, or new adventures, you slip on a certain style to get you in the right frame of mind. You aren't going to wear dress shoes to conquer a summit, but a new pair of Converse™ might give you an added rocker edge for your workday outfit. Every pair of shoes gives you the opportunity for a new mindset.

Think about it.

Shoes bring out the part of you needing to shine in that moment. It's not deception, but the chance to be you! We all have different roles, or in this case, why not call them *soles*? After all, we are talking about shoes! Those soles shine in *their* moments. Whether it's your sensitive side when a friend needs you most, or a confident side to show your leadership at work; it's all different facets of your personality. Only after just conquering this new adventure of running a marathon, was I ready to try on these next shoes and show that confident, leadership side of me to take it on.

Now, let's do some *sole* searching and become the person you have set out to be, taking on your next big challenge.

HERE IS YOUR FIRST TIP TO GET YOU STARTED:

★ *Put some shoes on those dreams!* Pick 4-5 styles of shoes or styles of the new you of how you see yourself in the next 10 years. Goals are dreams with boots on. Post pictures of them somewhere that are visible throughout the day. Some people call it a "vision board." I love to use a dry erase board. I love the versatility of it for writing, drawing and using magnets. I feel like new ideas are always formulating and I can quickly erase or add to it with different colors. However, you do it, visualizing you in your goal or living it, is very helpful to keep you focused on your target. Put pictures of you that show you living your dream already. Picture your future self…the clothes you are wearing, the environment you will be in. Give as much detail as possible. It is fun to create a vision board because, in the process, you are laying out the details to get there and your mind is more set on getting there.

CHAPTER 2

Dreaming the Possibilities

"It is not the mountain we conquer, but ourselves."

EDMUND HILLARY

Shoes help represent different stages or milestones in our lives. From when we first learned to walk to our first job, each momentous occasion had a special pair of shoes. One big milestone of my life happened when I was training for my first marathon.

Black combat boots.

I was seventeen when I considered wearing those boots. Those black, Grade-A boots made of leather were perfectly constructed and had a pristine shine. They were also the most uncomfortable shoes I'd worn so far in my life, but I knew breaking them in would be a new, exciting adventure. As I held them, I visualized the journeys I could have, taking on this new role. I wondered what experiences I would have, emotions I would feel, the people I would meet, the scuffs and lines that would create my stories. I felt as though these shoes also expected a lot out of me. There was a chance for big growth, and it was up to me to do it.

Have you ever visualized the possibilities when you get a new pair of shoes?

It's exciting and empowering to realize the adventures you *can* have. Now, did you notice I said "can" and not "will?" Just buying the shoes and visualizing the dream won't get you far, although very good first steps to take. You have to try them on and get moving!

One day during my senior year in high school, I saw a booth set up in the common area during my lunch break. It was for the Army National Guard. I started talking to the recruiter, asking simple questions about boot camp.

Aren't we all just a little curious about what really happens at boot camp? I was. Deep down, I even had the burning question, *"Could I hack boot camp?"* I wondered if I had what it took to make it through, and I wanted to know if all of the horror stories I'd seen on TV were true.

The recruiter answered my questions, sparking a good conversation, planting a seed of interest. As I began to see all of the potential benefits, it got the wheels turning in my mind. I had always disciplined myself with how I lived my life, so this seemed to fit.

I joined the Army National Guard 1/211 Aviation Unit on March 16, 2001, roughly five months after I approached the recruiting booth. I hadn't joined immediately because I wanted to make sure this was really the right path for me. My mom and I always had a pad of paper ready for whenever a question came about. Since this was a big decision, we wanted to make sure we asked everything we could.

I also had some anxieties that kept me from stepping into this new adventure immediately.

I knew this was going to be really hard.

Training to become a soldier was no "cush" life. I knew there would be sleepless nights and painful times that would push me more than anything I had ever done. That knowledge made me excited and terrified all at the same time. Hard things can prevent us from reaching bigger dreams and goals and stepping out of our comfort zone. Sometimes we are comfortable and what is wrong with that?

When I start to feel uncomfortable, my path must be wrong to pursue.

I'm always guilty of doubting the uncomfortable feeling. If I'm hitting roadblocks, then I must have to turn around, right? Some might say it's human nature, but it's up to us to break the stereotype! When I find myself getting uncomfortable, but I really believe in this goal, I try to go about it differently. If there's a roadblock, go around or jump over. If that doesn't work, then try something else. The end goal doesn't need to change, but we can find new ways to achieve it. We can rework the process to solve the problem, eventually meeting the end result.

I have found on those more uncomfortable, far-reaching, goals, the more I keep at it, the more habitual and easier it seems to pursue it. The process of reaching the goal becomes a part of me instead of an uncomfortable me.

There was a part of me that wanted to do something hard and knew that stepping out of my comfort zone was the only way to become someone better. I was now eager to step out of my old shoes into some very uncomfortable combat boots.

I was intrigued by what the Army could do for me, but also what I could do for the Army. I knew I could be a great soldier. I also saw the opportunity to gain an education and medical experience for my dream of being a nurse. There was opportunity for adventures, to serve and help so many people.

How could I not join?

I was always willing to serve my country, but my concept of "serving my country" was also very different at the time. I joined when there was no war going on. I was told my deployments would be for natural disasters and stateside situations. I was excited for such an opportunity to be a part of something that would make a difference in such a big way. Then, when our country was brutally attacked six months later, I knew my life would change. My concept of service to my country was completely altered. Though the unknown was always something that excited me, this was something I wasn't prepared for. Maybe I was in shock at first, but the more I thought about it, the more it terrified me. I thought of the Twin Towers crumbling to rubble, taking the lives of so many. It was suffocating the more I thought about the heartbreak. It took me a moment to gather my strength, but I soon took the heartbreak and I turned it into something I could use.

Now was my chance to help so many other people.

I shipped off to Basic Training in Fort Leonardwood, Missouri to train for war. We soldiers liked to call it "Fort

Lost-in-the-woods, Misery." That's where I trained to become a soldier, where I began my journey and service in those boots. It was a grueling three months of training. Most nights were teary-eyed and sleepless, testing my self-worth every time. I had to look back to the other shoes I had worn so far to help me realize what I had already overcome. I could do this, and there were a few lessons I learned in my scuffed-up boots.

WHY BLEND IN WHEN YOU WERE BORN TO STAND OUT?

I talked to a lot of soldiers before heading off to Basic Training, asking them questions and researching everything, so I knew what I was getting into. Among their many tips, was to blend in and not be noticed by the drill sergeants. The drill sergeants loved easy targets and making your life more miserable if you stood out. I wasn't expecting advice like that.

To blend in?

Not usually my style, plus it seemed too easy to blend in. Goodness, we all wore the exact same uniforms and had to have everything exactly the same from our appearance to our living quarters. How hard could it be?

We first arrived at Basic Training by cattle trucks, which was our most common mode of transportation. The trucks were filled with recruits from all across the country. We all looked so different from each other with our own story to tell, but it didn't matter anymore. We were now united in our purpose, as well as in our anxiety training to become soldiers. When the trucks finally stopped, we were all silent, not really sure what was going to happen next. The drill sergeants came screaming onto the trucks, demanding we get off and get into the building. We were all in a frantic panic, trying to make out their instructions through the screaming. There were dozens of drill sergeants handling the new recruits. They looked like they were out for blood as they screamed at us, like we were the scum under their shoes.

They were trying to break us.

As some privates were still running off the cattle trucks, others were already in formation, while the drill sergeants would pick us apart on any detail we weren't paying attention to. Some soldiers were already drawing attention to themselves—which I *knew not* to do, thanks to some great advice from my friends—by either moving too slowly or being clumsy in their scurry. The drill sergeants were not happy, and we soon found ourselves down in the "front leaning rest" position (a.k.a. push-ups).

"Welcome to your new home, privates," yelled one drill sergeant.

This was now our home for the next nine weeks, but it wasn't very welcoming. It was a three-story brick building, with each level consisting of a hallway of rooms and only two bathrooms. The first level was for the females, while the males took up the second and third floors. Each room had about four bunk beds with eight wall lockers. They then explained where each platoon needed to go and get "acquainted" with their drill sergeants (really just them yelling at us and showing us who's in charge).

My platoon's room was on the third floor. This was our *war room* where we would always meet together for PT, or physical training, and other instruction. The first day, we crammed in there with all of our bags, but not a word was spoken. Some privates were breathing hard, not only from exertion, but from fright as well. After ten minutes of us quietly sitting there, three drill sergeants walked into the room.

"At ease," we all yelled as we stood with our hands placed in the small of our back, which was the standard protocol when any non-commissioned officer of higher ranking, like a drill sergeant, walks into the room.

The three Drill Sergeants just stared at us, two males, Drill Sergeants Barto and Geiger, with one female, Drill Sergeant Dixon. I'd heard female sergeants were the worst, maybe because they had to prove to everyone, they weren't the "motherly-kind" and to not expect any slack from rules by them. They stood as tall as they could, yelling at us every chance they could as we stood in our lines. I couldn't remember what we did wrong, but it soon became a common theme—no matter what, we were always wrong. There wasn't too much room for them to walk, since there was about forty-five privates and all of our gear crammed into one small room, so they had us do "over-the-head claps" instead of push-ups.

The next few days were filled with more basic instruction as to what they expected of us. The fourth platoon was known as the, "War Lords." We were to yell that name every time we came to the position of attention as a platoon. It was name I would have never come up with on my own.

We had physical training twice a day, at least on the schedule. It didn't matter whether the day was meant for muscle training or running, our bodies were pushed to the limit and then some. Even though I loved the challenge, it needed all the mental and physical strength I had, so I took advantage of every second I could, promising myself I would never give up. I fought through every sit-up, push-up, and distance run even while others caved. I wanted to show the drill sergeant I was a hard worker and could be counted on. I didn't want to blend in when I knew I was meant to stand out.

With our first physical training test on the horizon, I felt confident I would succeed. The goal was to track our physicality then and see how much we would improve over the training period. Though the drill sergeants didn't count reps like they should, many suggested it would be easier to hold back and save my energy for the ending test, I didn't have the heart to take the easy way out.

I always gave it my all.

Three recruits were being graded at a time and it was now my turn. My body already burned from the week of training, but I found it in me to keep going strong. I strained to hear the drill sergeant call out what number I was on through my push-ups, and I almost collapsed in shock when he only said I'd done seven! I knew I had done at least twenty by the end of the time limit. Even sit-ups, I did at least fifty but was only counted thirty-five.

Once the two-mile run came along, though, I was confident they couldn't cheat my time.

I loved the two-mile run because I knew I could do it, but I also hated it at the same time. It was a sprint compared to what my body was used to from the marathons. I finished, but it was nowhere near the time I was hoping for. I wondered what had slowed me down. Was it the weather? The physical exhaustion my body was facing?

Even though it was a slower-than-average time for me, I still ended up as one of the top finishers, not only in my platoon, but in my company. I was really surprised! Weren't people who joined the Army already physically fit?

I couldn't have been more wrong. For a majority of my company and many others within the military, joining the Army was the first time they started working out. Many privates were injured within the first few weeks of training and put on a profile, which meant they couldn't do certain activities in physical training because of an injury. I vowed from the very beginning I would never be one of those soldiers.

From my experience, if you're fit, you stick out in the military and are more respected because of what you can do. Being fit definitely helped me throughout my military career, but I was still in the minority by being fit.

Word got around about my training results, giving me an advantage. Our scores determined our run groups: Alpha for high-speed runners, Bravo for the decently paced, and Charlie for those who weren't made for running, but made to do it. The final group was Delta, for the "broken" and injured. If you were in Delta very long you were either kicked out or moved to another company. In other words, their training would take a lot longer than nine weeks. As the only female in Alpha, I was thankful for not ever holding myself back, giving me the advantage I needed.

We had three more physical training tests throughout the nine weeks. I always tried to exceed my previous scores, earning the nicknames "PT" and "PT 5000." With my scoring among the top recruits, I kept pushing myself to stay there, and even the drill sergeants were rooting for me.

Some of my comrades struggled with the physical training test, so I volunteered to help. I offered to pace them when they were given another opportunity to pass. I loved being able to help them have the chance to graduate.

As the weeks went on, our "smoking" sessions (punishment for when we're in trouble) became more individualized instead of as a whole platoon, which was a relief, giving our bodies a little break. I soon gained a new reputation, that if any girl needed a battle buddy (because we always had to have a battle buddy with anything) when they were in trouble, to ask me. I received questionable looks from some of the drill sergeants when they would see me getting smoked with a battle buddy multiple times a day. I used it to get stronger, trying to make things as positive as possible.

Turns out, those who excelled in physical training were put into leadership roles in the platoon, and I was made a Squad Leader after the first test. Even though I was told to *blend in* and leaders at Basic Training are set up for failure many times, I was glad I pushed myself to stand out. I could have held myself back and still technically passed the tests, but why just get by? Why not see what your potential is in each shoe? I was already fit, but I knew I could be faster and stronger. *Yes*, I did draw attention to myself to get picked on more, but that didn't last long because eventually, they wanted my help.

Trying to stand out and doing my best at every chance paid off each time.

In the end, I earned the Highest Physical Fitness Award for my company and went on to improve my scores even more in my Combat Medic Training, earning the Highest Physical Fitness Award there as well. Never hold yourself back and blend in when you were born to stand out!

OVERCOMING DOUBT/VISUALIZING SUCCESS

One of my least favorite drills during my military training was the gas chamber. I understood why it was important, but I hated it! The day before our turn in the chamber, we were fitted for our masks. To get the right fit, you had to be able to create a seal on the mask against your face so no gas could leak through.

As we shuffled into the dark, smoky room, I had no idea what to expect, and it terrified me. At least I wasn't feeling anything unusual, which meant I had a good seal on my mask.

When the drill sergeant came around, approaching each soldier, we had to break the seal on our mask to recite our name, rank, and unit. They wanted to see we weren't holding our breath. When I lifted up my mask, I immediately felt a burning sensation on my skin, feeling the burn travel all the way down my airway into my lungs. I hacked out my name, rank, and unit, and as soon as I was done reciting, I was allowed to reseal the mask. I still felt like I was inhaling the gas, and I wanted to get out of there. They do this because you're only in the gas chamber for a few minutes and some soldiers have the talent of holding their breath for that long (I sure don't).

When you're in chemical warfare, you could be exposed to chemicals for hours, even days. They want to make sure you learn to trust your mask so you're prepared to handle unexpected situations in the future. We were allowed to leave the chamber, but if we were caught running out, we would have to go back in. I hoped that after that day, I was finished with the gas training.

During one of our last events, we were camping out in the mountains, where we got lots of training and very little sleep. One morning, we were awakened by a loud pop followed by a hissing sound. We all new that sound too well—the drill sergeants had released a gas grenade a few feet from where we were all attempting to sleep. I quickly grabbed my mask, putting it on as the air got cloudy around me. In my haste, I wasn't sure if my mask had sealed properly, causing me to doubt if I was adequately protected. Just like in life, no matter how much you try to prepare, there's always a doubt in the back of your mind, questioning if you had done enough.

As I was trying to run away from the fog of chemicals, I wasn't feeling any symptoms of exposure yet, so I thought I was safe. But as I continued to run, I could feel my mask bouncing slightly, slipping off my face. Sweat started to sting my skin, and my eyes burned along with my nose. I could see the inside of my mask was starting to get cloudy, blocking my view even more. I ran blindly through the forest trying to dodge not only the gas but the trees. I fell to the ground hard, tripping over a branch. As I fell, my mask broke completely loose. My battle buddies finally found me and helped drag me out of the forest, coughing and gasping for air. Let's just say I learned my lesson to not only trust in my equipment and training, but to know I am better capable when calm. I planned to never repeat that mistake.

As I trained in the Army, I learned that fear can be a great motivator. It's the Army's main tactic to weed out the "weak." *Survival of the fittest, right?* There are many dangerous things that can cause fear for a soldier. If we don't already have confidence in our equipment like our gas masks, battle buddies, and especially ourselves, it can threaten our abilities. So, it makes sense to use fear in our training so we are confident and ready for what dangerous things we may face. Yet, fear isn't always the best way to discover or develop your strengths.

Training and challenges help you build trust within yourself, no matter the situation. From my shoes, if I had just trusted my equipment, I would have been fine. Doubt is a form of fear. I doubted myself and doubted the mask being enough, running away and making it a reality.

When we allow negative thoughts to creep into our minds, our vision is clouded, and we lose focus of our goals. We get scared. We start to wonder if this goal was a little too big to achieve. The thought often comes to mind, "Maybe I should change my goal, make it a little easier" or "Maybe I wasn't cut out for this and need to try something else." These thoughts soon become how you feel, then show through your actions, making it a reality.

"Thoughts and opinions aren't good or bad, right or wrong, as they enter your mind, but they sure can be empowering or disempowering to your happiness and success, as they enter your life."

T. HARV EKER,
SECRETS OF A MILLIONAIRE MIND.

Let's consider something simple like running a mile. Your thoughts might change and decide the mile is too long, to a half a mile, to barely making a few feet, then eventually, you just stop trying. All because of your opinion or outlook of it. By making your goals smaller each time, you're changing your mindset, and you lose faith in who you are. Adding some smaller steps to get you to your goal is great and sometimes needed. You don't need to change your goal just your plan of attack.

It takes practice.

The more you do it, the more empowered you will be as you refocus your thoughts to support your vision. Don't waste your energy on the problems and doubts because it won't get you anywhere. If you want to improve your life, improve your thinking. This has been proven time and time again in my life and many others.

Why not yours?

BECOMING SOLDIERS:

Finally, it came down to our culminating event... our FTX, or field training exercise. We spent days camping out in a field, rolling around in the mud, sleeping in bitter cold foxholes, and being woken by gas grenades.

Those were the longest days of my life!

The last day of FTX was the toughest. We packed everything up, cleared the area, and began our march home, yet we weren't told how long it was going to be. We were already hurting after these last few days of training in the cold. Physically and emotionally exhausted, we were in full battle attire with all our gear, making two lines on each side of the road. After a couple hours, many were struggling to keep up, being passed by other soldiers. Though they had trucks for those who were injured, the idea teased us as like a mirage in the desert. Everyone was struggling, even myself. As much as I tried to help, I could barely put one foot in front of the other to help myself.

This march seemed never ending. Hours went by before we finally stumbled into an open field. It was another range.

We had been to dozens of these already! Zeroing in on your weapon is one of the main skills of being a soldier, and we went to a lot of ranges developing that skill, shooting at different pop-up targets, but this was different. It was actually *live-fire* being shot at us. We were told we had better be crawling as low as we could get so not to get hit. The shots had tracers on them so you could see them in the dark. It looked like something out of a Star Wars™ movie as colorful lights shot above us and loud explosions went off everywhere else.

Our drill sergeants tried to create a combat zone similar to what we might face as soldiers in the field. I sure felt like I had already been through one. Crawling low with all our gear on the hard, rocky ground really tested my strength. I was in so much pain as I inched forward, rocks cutting into my skin, so I tried to shift my weight to find a better way of crawling. No matter what I did, it hurt. My emotions were coming on strong, and I felt I truly couldn't take it anymore. I'd had enough! My chest and throat were burning as I tried to hold back tears. Drill sergeants were yelling at us everywhere while more shots and explosions fired. This was the night they separated the strong from the weak.

After crawling a few hundred yards, we formed up at the other end. Our battalion commander met us there to initiate us. Our whole company gathered there—well, what was left of us. We were a sight for sore eyes, but we made it. Some had tear stains on their cheeks, washing off some of the dirt we were layered with. Our uniforms were drenched with sweat and stained with blood, when we formed up to listen to our battalion commander.

I had now earned the title of soldier.

My combat boots, now well broken in, showed the scuffs and stories I had just overcome, including the lessons I learned and skills I discovered about myself. Take a look at the scuffs on your shoes and see what you have overcome already.

You were born to shine!

In the Army we have a phrase we use in combat—lock 'n load! It means to be ready for anything and not waste your ammo, making every shot count. I've taken this meaning to heart in all aspects of my life. It's my motto. I realize it's important for anyone living in this world—to make every shot count—so don't waste this one shot at life to shine. Lock 'n load!

There may be times when you doubt whether following this goal is a good idea. Never stop trying to clear those bad thoughts out and zeroing in on your goal. Rachel Hollis tells us, "You'll teach yourself a new way to behave and set a standard for the type of person you truly are." You will become unstoppable as you fill your thoughts and your shoes with things to help you step forward.

TIPS FROM THIS CHAPTER:

★ *Reflect* and look at all you have done so far, the scuffs on yours shoes. Realize what you have already overcome and learned already.

★ *Improve your thinking.* The whole list of anxieties you saw at the beginning is caused by our own selves. When a thought comes into your mind that brings you down or makes you second guess, you tear that thought up and throw it out. Look at your goals you have written down, your vision board to help you reset. Have thoughts that build you up.

★ When you get uncomfortable or it's getting hard, don't make your goals smaller, just *change your approach.*

CHAPTER 3

I'm Not Ready to Wear these Shoes Yet

The shoes we don't think we can fill

"What we fear doing most is usually what we most need to do."

RALPH WALDO EMERSON

Life is good, right? Everything is going just as you pictured it would be. Then, without warning, you're handed shoes you just don't see how you could possibly wear. This happened to me while continuing my studies in nursing school. Things were going quite well for me, living the college life. Then, without warning, I was handed a new pair of shoes. Shoes I didn't want to wear because deep down, I didn't really think I could.

Have you ever been handed a pair of shoes you felt you couldn't fill? We all have! You may be in denial about it, but you have. A tragedy happens, perhaps the loss of a loved one, a medical prognosis that doesn't look so good, losing your job—the list can go on. Life is full of surprises and some of them are hard to take.

FAITH IN THE UNKNOWN

The holidays were approaching, and as any college student would admit, it's a needed break you look forward to among the demands of studies. While on my road trip home, I was daydreaming about spending Thanksgiving with my family and the fun traditions we had. I loved baking with my mom, breaking out in song with all my siblings while working in the kitchen, even playing in the family Turkey Bowl.

However, I got a call from my section sergeant during my four-hour drive home. The call wasn't unexpected—I received one every month, informing me about drill schedules. The next one was planned for December, and it was going to be our Christmas party, but this time my sergeant didn't sound very cheerful.

"Um, sorry, Stevens. Plans have changed," she said. "You have to be here in a couple of weeks. We're going to Afghanistan."

Silence.

I couldn't speak.

I couldn't breathe.

"Okay, have a happy Thanksgiving," I tried to say.

I was alone in my car as I tried calling friends and family with the news, but no one answered. My emotions rose, mostly of fear and anger.

I needed to talk to someone!

During the next few hours, I ended up having a good one-on-one chat with God. "What is going on? Why are you doing this to me?" I asked. I had everything going for me. This couldn't possibly be right.

What good could possibly come from this?

After a good hour or so of pouring out my feelings and crying until my tear ducts were dry, I changed my prayers from asking why me, why now to now asking for help. I needed him to give me the strength to get through this journey. Just when I thought all hope was lost, I remembered a song written by my mother. It felt like God was answering my prayers. The song compared our lives to a tapestry.

I do not know the pattern or design of what I do

Or the end of this great work that is for me.

Still I weave with care each day,

Every color on my way

And trust he'll guide what only he can see.

This masterpiece of love, my tapestry.

I remember being a little girl, listening to her angelic voice singing me to sleep with her songs. Little did I know, those songs would teach me important lessons and carry me later on in life. Sometimes, we are only looking at the side of the tapestry with all of the knots, strings, and entanglements. Just like those imperfections, I was angry at God for putting me through this, but the Lord is looking at something far more beautiful on the other side. That's what it comes down to, faith. The belief that your life will come together as it was meant to, even when your handed circumstances that are painful and difficult to navigate, you become something far greater on the other side of that mountain.

I knew I needed to place my trust in Him. It should bring comfort to all of us; no matter how uncomfortable the shoe may be, knowing that God has a purpose for us. Now, I know why the Lord needed me over in Afghanistan—to learn what I needed to for myself, then help others through their hard times.

So many overwhelming feelings of doubt and fear still entered my mind, even after accepting this challenge. I needed to put into practice what I had learned in my previous shoes. Now, it was time to don my desert combat boots.

Was I ready to go to combat? Had I done everything I could to be the kind of soldier I needed to be?

I needed to believe I had. I needed to visualize and believe in my mind that all I had accomplished so far was to prepare me for these hard times.

I completed a lot of hard tasks before, like running a marathon and making it through basic training, so I knew I could take on anything that came my way. After weeks of refocusing my mind, I found an exercise to get me through this tough time.

Think and list the positives in my life and about this event.

I didn't want to list pros and cons. Those types of lists work really well if you have a choice about doing something. In the case of being called to war, I didn't. I had to go. So why list out and focus on the bad? Listing out the positive and even carrying the list with me to remind myself when my thoughts got negative, helped me keep the right frame of mind. This exercise is simple, but helps to be optimistic when you are handed shoes in life that take you by surprise and you have to go through with it.

My feelings of doubt were now fading. Some fear was still there, but that was normal. What was more important was where my thoughts and energy were now focused. I felt empowered, and I dare say, excited to start this adventure.

I had faith in this new path.

KEEPING YOUR EYE ON THE TARGET

As a soldier, we are trained on many different types of weapons, going to many different shooting ranges to practice. Most of our ranges consisted of pop-up targets 50 to 300 yards away. One day, we went to a new range, in preparation for Afghanistan. It was a close-fire range, where we were only about twenty-five feet from the target. Instead of lying on the ground and shooting, we would go through different walking and pivoting motions, simulating combat before facing our target. I figured this was going to be a piece of cake with the target that close.

I went in a group of about twenty soldiers where we stood in a line in front of our own targets. We practiced pivoting before turning to shoot, modeling real combat situations.

After shooting only three shots, we would check our targets. I still remember the excitement I had running up to my target thinking I just nailed it. Little did I know, not one of my shots touched.

I thought, *you've got to be kidding me! I'm about to go to war and I can't even shoot something twenty-five feet in front of me?*

I checked other soldiers' targets next to mine. They were actually hitting the paper, but were still way off from hitting the silhouette. When I looked at my friend Hamilton's target (a medic I served with), which was right next to mine. I saw three holes grouped together right in the chest. He definitely had an advantage being a member of the S.W.A.T. team in Utah prior to training for the Army National Guard.

After seeing my results, I pleaded with Hamilton to help me out. With little convincing, he agreed, considering I was going to be fighting right next to him. The next round, after Hamilton advised me on how to hold my hand steady and take a deep breath before shooting, I checked the target and found three holes grouped tightly together on the target. I did a complete double-take and cheered while doing a little victory dance.

All of the soldiers were just shaking their heads and smiling, but Hamilton was busting up with laughter. I figured he must have been so proud of me, but he continued to laugh. It just didn't seem right to me. He should be congratulating his newfound apprentice, not laughing at me! Once he regained his composure, he said, "Stevens, I'm sorry, but that was me shooting at your target just to see your reaction. Man, was it worth it!"

"You didn't!" I fired back. I cringed at those words. Please tell me he didn't just say that. So, I responded, "Prove it!"

So, we decided to both shoot at the same target. Hamilton aimed for the right shoulder and me aiming for the left. The results? Let's just say it's a good thing I'm a medic and not in the infantry. Talk about going from an all-time high to an all-time low in just a couple of minutes.

By the end of the day, I got better at my aim but I still wasn't the best at that particular target practice. I do know having a goal, or target, is essential in all aspects of life though, but we can be knocked off course, causing us to lose focus.

How real is your target? Is it far away or close up? Does it just pop-up when you feel like taking a casual shot at it? Or are you focused and ready, taking those steps to pivot around and get closer to your goal?

It was no different for me when I was called to serve in Afghanistan. It could have been a terrible sixteen months away from home; a rotten interruption in my education and goals I set for my career, and a worrisome time for my family. Not to mention it was a scary situation for me as a soldier helping to fight the war on terrorism. Instead, I tried to set goals of what I wanted to accomplish, then worked to keep my target in view. I took my desert combat boots and visualized, as best I could (since I had never been to Afghanistan, let alone war), what I wanted my year to look like.

How did I want to show up? I pictured myself doing my job as a medic, taking care of soldiers, and doing it well. I pictured making others happy around me, because

Afghanistan didn't seem like the happiest place to go, so why not try to bring a little cheer? I pictured myself being proud of the impact I could make protecting the innocent people in Afghanistan caught in the mindless war. And then, I pictured what it would feel like when I got home having done my best, then worked backwards from there.

It happens to all of us as we set out on life's journey. We need to be living each day to the fullest and going after big dreams, embracing the change in your plans. By visualizing and focusing on what you want to accomplish in the end, your mind will fill in the gaps along the way.

We all face different challenges in life. Some stresses can distract you, making you lose sight of your target. The important thing is staying focused at all times on the end goal. Focusing will help you be that much more determined to succeed and hit the difficult target you set for yourself.

As I was aiming for mine, here were some steps along the way that really helped me accomplish what I set out to do and I know they will help you too.

1. Fill your shoes your own way.
2. Surround yourself with the "good."
3. Never turn down an opportunity to learn more.
4. Scuff up others' "soles" with service.

FILL YOUR SHOES YOUR OWN WAY

I served as a medic for an Aviation Unit in Bagram, Afghanistan, taking care of soldiers' needs. I mainly worked in a little hut, we called our Aid Station, that ran much like an Urgent Care setting in the States. I would also go on flights in

Blackhawks and Chinooks (a larger helicopter), supporting soldiers on their different missions. After a couple of months of my boots on ground, serving in combat on these missions, I discovered a life-changing and eye-opening lesson.

While taking care of these soldiers, fixing their physical injuries, I felt there was more to be done, more than just mending their battle wounds or illnesses. There was the emotional side. When morale was low, missions were harder to perform and became less successful. We've all been through those low moments in our lives where our attentiveness was lacking and we tended to drag our feet. Some points in our lives, just like those missions in Afghanistan, needed our full attention, as lives depended on it. So, I thought I could help.

I found a new way to fill my shoes.

I didn't have to be like every other soldier, and at first, I was trying to do that. That's why fear and doubt crept into my mind. I was comparing myself to all the incredible soldiers who have worn these boots, but I wasn't like them. As we take on different challenges, we can get blindsided by comparing ourselves with others doing the same thing but you need to know that you bring your own uniqueness to that circumstance. The other soldiers brought different skills, filling their boots their own way. I could fill my boots in my own unique way, and I found lots of ways to do so.

I became a morale booster in every way I could. I would randomly stop by tents, offices or aviation hangars to check up on soldiers and say "hi." I baked in Afghanistan, too. We had electricity over there, so I had my mom send me a bread machine. Whenever I heard a soldier was having a rough day, or maybe their birthday was coming up, I would bake them a fresh, homemade loaf of bread or cake.

You thought the smell of homemade bread in your kitchen was a trip to your senses? Try it on soldiers in a combat zone. It's priceless!

Word traveled fast about what I was doing, and I soon got orders from different company commanders to make bread for soldiers in their unit who were going through tough times. I was glad to be of help, finding a positive way to fill my shoes.

I then tried to do more. I began planning parties for special occasions, game nights, and even a "girls' night out" once in a while.

Decorating for holidays became a great way to fill my shoes differently and involve soldiers to get their minds off being in a combat zone. I painted rocks to look like pumpkins, setting them out in front of our Aid Station at the beginning of October. Soon, other soldiers became caught up in the Halloween spirit too, creating new scenarios for the pumpkins each day. They dealt cards to each pumpkin to look like they are playing a game, created a school class, and had an injured pumpkin on a stretcher (my personal favorite), creating some fun during some dire situations. Soldiers around the base would make sure to pass by our Aid Station to see what the pumpkins were up to that day.

Thanksgiving became another way to boost morale. I know most families try to focus more on gratitude by setting up a thankful tree or bowl to share their thoughts—at least that's what I grew up doing. I loved the tradition and wanted to continue it in Afghanistan. Some days were harder than others, to prove to the soldiers there was still something to be grateful for, but I helped nudge them along with some ideas to keep their perspective positive. Our thankful tree grew every day and was a great reminder to us daily. Many soldiers often walked by to see how it grew. Baking, planning parties, and decorating for holidays might not sound like soldier things or war things in the way we typically view them, but I found them necessary. It was a calling, if you will, to bring hope and happiness to a place that seemed hopeless.

With different shoes we wear, we tend to compare ourselves to someone else who is wearing the same, or similar, shoes. They might make it look easier or excel at what you seem to be struggling with, just as I compared myself to the incredible soldiers I served with. You don't have to be like them though. Fill your shoes in your own unique way. The world needs more you, just like Bagram Air Base needed someone like me.

SURROUND YOURSELF WITH GOOD

To keep myself focused on our mission as well as my personal goals of how I can contribute, I wanted to surround myself with things that built me up. That not only meant the people I hung out with but the things I placed in my room. Granted, some things were a less accessible in a combat zone, but it didn't need to stop me.

My walls were wooden due to living in huts, making them easy to change, so I felt why not write on them? I hung pictures of people I looked up to. I wrote close to one hundred inspiring quotes and scriptures on the walls and even the ceiling to help me during times I felt down.

Wait, what? I was down sometimes? Even the famous Morale Booster of Bagram Air Base fell on hard times. As much as I tried to fight it, sometimes those doubts came rolling in at full force.

Besides missing family, friends, and the comforts of living back in the states, there were harder days along with some soldiers that I butted heads with. Our personalities weren't a good match.

In many circumstances, it can be beneficial to cut ties with people who bring you down. I had no choice but to work with them. You want to surround yourself with people who build you up or you serve to build up. I couldn't be reassigned, so my room became my sanctuary. It was my place to feel peace and to rebuild myself after days I was torn down. Even after giving it my best, there was always something I couldn't measure up to with the leader I struggled with. I could have let these people ruin my experience in Afghanistan, but I chose not to let them. I placed myself in positive environments as much as I could. When you are actively engaged and choosing to enjoy your own life, it doesn't really matter where you are, even if your life does feel like a battle zone and negative things get hurled at you.

You can still find happiness! It's not about where you are or what you have but *who you are* each step of the way.

NEVER TURN DOWN AN OPPORTUNITY TO LEARN MORE

Being in Afghanistan for a year, I could have had a bad attitude. I could have focused on the "poor me" approach, plugging along, doing the bare minimum to get by. *Goodness, that sounded miserable just writing that!* It would've been a terrible downward spiral to get into.

I wanted to make the most of this year. I didn't know if I would be deployed to Afghanistan again, so why not learn all I could? Whenever someone needed help, or commanders were asking for volunteers on a mission or a certain task, I raised my hand. I *wanted* to be that person. At the beginning of the year, I made a choice to make this experience great, instead of waiting for someone else to do it for me. Not only did I have an incredible adventure, but I learned more than I could ever imagine.

Even though my assignment was being part of the Aid Station on slower days, I was always trying to see if other medical facilities needed help. It was my eagerness that landed me great learning opportunities, not only the US Army Hospital (a whole hospital set up with tents), but in Korean and Egyptian hospitals on base as well. I got to scrub-in on surgeries, assist in operations, and learn about acupuncture. I even had it performed on me by one of the Korean doctors! I worked side-by-side Egyptian nurses, finding we had so much in common. They not only became dear friends, but I learned about how incredible those women were as well.

Another opportunity arose when we got word more help was needed on another base in Kandahar. Things were getting more dangerous, so another medic and I volunteered to help provide medical personnel on missions.

July 1, 2001: Another month down and another great month this next one has started out to be with a move to a new base. Today was a good day! I got to go on my first mission outside the gate in Kandahar. I volunteered myself to assist two other females helping the local women. Only females are allowed to help females. We had a small room for them in one of the Afghan buildings in the village Haji Tuti, only around eight to ten miles from our post in Kandahar. When the women came in, they were allowed to take off their burkas to the point of showing their face.

Our female interpreter named Sarah helped us tremendously. We couldn't have done it without her! The women seemed so innocent, all so beautiful in their own way. As you look at them, you can tell they have so much culture living inside them. Some of them look very similar to the people I've seen in the states, but these women were suffering. Their living conditions were terrible, and they were forced into a culture that treated them poorly. How they live is heartbreaking. A woman was put in prison for fourteen days because she shook someone's hand. Others because they spoke when they weren't supposed to, or looked at someone (uncovering their face), etc.

I feel so sorry for these women. I want so badly to give them a better life, to show them their worth, and that they are daughters of God, precious and loved. I was saddened at the thought I had to turn some of the women down when they asked for medical help because we had to go. We were just doing basic care for fevers, colds, aches and pains, cuts, skin care, etc. Some would come in with crying babies asking for something to help. We were definitely trying everything we could, but it didn't seem to be enough.

After a few more weeks in Kandahar supporting the missions, it was time to head back home to the base. Yet, what I saw in Kandahar and how I felt being among the people stayed with me. I wanted to help them, to give them the care they needed. I wasn't the only one who wanted to help these people in a non-militant way. Other soldiers in my unit shared this same desire of wanting to do more. In small ways, we were already bringing them medical attention, which was a start, but we needed to do more. It wasn't until I met Layne Pace, an officer with determination, that we finally got somewhere. The Army threw constant obstacles in his path, slowing him down, but it didn't stop him. He always found a way to better someone's life, and I wanted to be on the same team fighting for that cause.

There were many ways we performed the humanitarian services, once we knew who to talk to. It started small with local villages near the base but grew to remote areas across the country. I became similar to a medical representative, participating in the Humanitarian Committee along with Pace and a few others.

We involved a lot of our families back in the U.S. to help us collect necessary items and ship them over. We expected lots of shipments to be made with items like medical and dental supplies, school supplies, clothes, shoes, candy, and hygiene items. I was so excited to be part of such goodness! Little did I know how much one village would soon impact my life.

Jegdalek.

Pace learned about a village called Jegdalek, which was one we decided to adopt, considering they were really suffering from a lack of resources. We did many humanitarian missions and a few of those also included medical services. We met with the Elders of the village to get acquainted with them. We wanted to show them we were there to help, not only for that visit, but future visits as well. Our interpreter, Shah, was kind enough to help translate, giving us the opportunity to share our knowledge and really help them in the best way possible.

While on these missions, we filled half of the Chinook with large pallets of products. We landed on top of a hill in Jegdalek, ready to share items like clothes, supplies, and of course, shoes, with the village.

While on these missions, many soldiers were simply there to do their duty and perform the minimum. Now, don't get me wrong, I was too. Yet when I landed, I was eager to do more. I wanted to learn all I could about their culture among the people.

I spent most of my time with the kids. At first, it was difficult to communicate with them, speaking completely different languages and growing up in different parts of the world. I prayed to find ways to connect with them to try to have fun positive memories together, learning and playing with them. As we sat together, we ended up creating our own games (some version of tag or charades at times) and really bonded, learning more about each other through our shared ideas.

Whatever cards you're dealt in life, you have a choice to make the most out of the experience. How great the situation turns out is not up to others, but up to you. This is an ongoing skill to always keep building on, no matter what shoes you are wearing or ones you are dealt without warning.

WALKING A MILE IN SOMEONE ELSE'S SHOES

When I first landed in Afghanistan, the first question I had was, where do I run?

Running was the part of life my soul craved. It was like an itch that needed to be scratched. It was the one thing giving me the confidence no matter where I was in the world.

After asking around, I finally got an answer from one of the more experienced soldiers. He told me about a six-mile route, which sounded amazing!

The only catch?

The path wove through a minefield.

That week I decided to risk it. Probably not one of my brightest moments, but when you want to run, you have to go for it! It was a rocky dirt path—just like the rest of the country—with barbed-wire fences, only five-feet on either side with red, triangular signs every few feet that read, "MINES." *Again*, not my brightest moment, but the odds seemed to be in my favor since I came back with all my limbs attached.

During our deployment, some soldiers decided to have the first marathon in Afghanistan. News traveled fast, and as a runner, it was something I couldn't pass up on.

It felt nice to have another challenge to focus on; it kept my spirits high. This was the toughest marathon I'd ever done. It was a marathon just to get to the starting line!

We flew in the middle of the night, carrying all of our combat gear, barely getting any sleep. After many delays of trying to secure a helicopter to take us the rest of the way (flights were always changing in the strategy of different missions), we finally landed two hours before the race started so we could get briefed on all the safety precautions. I was excited, exhausted, and scared silly, all at the same time.

In order to run the full 26.2 miles, the route took us five laps through a rocky trail around the parameter of the base. I started strong through four laps, but the last lap had me really questioning why I had willingly chosen to run another marathon. So, many questions came to mind, but there was only one that mattered.

What did I need to prove to myself?

After starting up the last hill, it felt like torture. I began doubting my ability to finish the race, because I was both mentally and physically exhausted. Then, the impact of what I was really doing hit me.

I was a woman, running in a country where other women were degraded and demoralized.

I was here, free and striving to be better than I was yesterday. Through a rush of anger and frustration for the women of Afghanistan, I then felt a sense of pride. I was proud to be an American woman, and even more proud to be an American soldier fighting for those women and their worth.

A sudden drive came over me, carrying me through to the finish. With every step, the thought of those beautiful women pushed me to not give up. I did it for them.

Could I ever really walk a mile in their shoes? *Never.* Yet, at that moment and during other missions serving them, I felt I was on the sidelines of their race, cheering them on. I was helping them change the stories in their shoes, and even providing shoes for those who didn't even have any.

We are given opportunities in life where we get to help or influence someone else, creating memories and scuff marks on their shoes, hopefully for the better. In reality, they end up leaving bigger marks on our own *soles.*

On one of our first missions to Jegdalek, we noticed a little girl around the age of five playing with us and all of the other kids just after we handed out supplies. Her name was Halima. I remember this bold girl climbing onto my lap when I sat down. She was so cute and fun. We giggled and teased each other, but we also noticed there was a problem with her eyes. Later, we found out she had a severe case of congenital esotropia, a lack of muscle control of each eye, making it difficult to see at times in both eyes, but it never seemed to slow her down.

When we flew back to Bagram, days later, we reviewed our mission and found pictures of Halima. Remembering this spunky girl, we realized she'd left an impression on us. One colonel mentioned the possibility of fixing her eyes. Within a couple of days and a lot of phone calls, we had it all worked out with a U.S. and Egyptian eye surgeon on base. A flight quickly scheduled to pick her up, the only catch was that no one in her village knew about our plans.

We arrived in Jegdalek and started talking to the Elders of the village. It took a couple of hours, but once Halima and her father found out we were taking them to get her eyes fixed, they went home to change into her nicest dress. They were with us for the next week while she healed. Though I was her medical caregiver, I liked to see it more as her big sister.

We treated her like a queen. The day after she arrived, we took her to what we soldiers nicknamed, the "Bagram Day Spa," although it was really just a basic hair salon, it made her feel special. It was right on base and was run by Russian/Kyrgyzstan women to give them employment opportunities. They didn't know very much English, but they helped cut soldiers' hair when needed. We went there to get Halima's hair washed, but she ended up leaving with a cute hairstyle, manicure, and pedicure. The women were so excited to have a little girl in the salon instead of another sweaty soldier. Halima was expressionless throughout the whole thing. I'm sure it was a very different experience for her, but we got a bright smile out of her every once in a while.

September 7, 2004: Halima's surgery went well. Both the Egyptian and U.S. eye doctors operated on an eye. After two days of recovery, we took her the next day, and I picked out a cute new pink dress and gave her a shower. I think we built a strong, trusting relationship with her and her father that week. My goodness, she looked adorable...a true Cinderella story! She is a very obedient girl. She just always let us do what we wanted with her. We even watched Cinderella later that day (of course!). I believe she liked it, even though she didn't understand any of it, because she busted into laughter whenever the mice were shown. It was such a great week! This has made my whole deployment worthwhile! I started calling her "my little Cinderella" from then on.

Though Halima struggled to see, she never let it get her down. She overcame her adversities, and in the end, we were able to help her. Just like with Halima, we are handed shoes, challenges in life that hold us back from letting our true selves shine out. But, just like Halima, we can still see the good that surrounds us.

When we flew her and her father back to Jegalek, their village was excited to see them and hear about their week with us. We soon said goodbye and expected to see each other in a few weeks, which is when we were usually able to get back to Jegdalek. Months went by as other missions were more critical at the time and I wondered if I was ever going to be able to make it back to see these wonderful people again before our deployment was over.

Finally, we were able to secure a mission back after being away for so long. I was so worried the kids would forget me after five months of being away. When we got there, I put down my bags and headed over to where the crowds were gathered by the containers of supplies. All of the kids were so excited to see me, calling out my name. It was like music to my ears!

They actually remembered who I was! It was wonderful to see some familiar faces and especially the small group of young girls that seemed to follow my every move when I was there.

As I played with the young girls, making silly faces and singing songs, I noticed something was missing. Though the entire village had a special place in my heart, there was one little girl that I grew so closely with after our time together.

Halima.

After a few hours, I still hadn't seen Halima yet. A sick feeling hit me as I wondered if she was okay. Was she still alive? If you haven't seen someone for a while in that country, you couldn't help but wonder if something has happened to them. I prayed she was all right. It was just about time for us to leave when the kids around me started calling out, "Halima, Halima!"

I flipped around, and I swear what happened next couldn't have been produced better in a movie—the crowds parted, and here came Halima running straight towards me with arms wide open. We did one of those hugs where I picked her up and swung her around, and I swore I heard music in the background. I was almost in tears as I held her in my arms.

When Halima ran up to me and wrapped her arms around me, I knew every sacrifice I made to be in their country was worth it. Having that five-year old girl run up to me like we were sisters was priceless. I realized this was why I was there— to make a difference in her life with her old, barely holding together sandals, and have her make a difference in mine, with my dusty combat boots. That was one moment I would never forget as I looked at the scuff marks of my boots.

"God has perfect timing, and it's highly possible that by not being where you thought you should be, you will end up exactly where you're meant to go."

RACHEL HOLLIS, GIRL, WASH YOUR FACE

TIME TO SAY GOODBYE

After a couple more missions, our time in Afghanistan was coming to a close. It was finally time to say goodbye. That's when it hit me: I would never see these kids again! I got a little choked up, even though I thought, *Soldiers don't cry! There's no crying in the Army!* It soon became impossible not to.

The girls gathered around me, and I was trying to let them know I was going back to America and would never see them again. I could tell they didn't understand. One girl kept repeating what I said, but in the end, it didn't matter. I gave them all a hug and they gave one back, which was something I needed.

As I started walking up the hill to the landing zone, I took one last look back at the girls that had changed my life. All it took was that one look as I let the tears stream down my face. I knew I would miss them terribly.

When we loaded into the aircraft, all the soldiers sat in silence, not wanting to believe that something we worked so hard for was now coming to an end. Yes, we were excited to get home to see our families, but we were sad to leave the new family we had grown so close to in the past year.

Then one soldier broke the silence and whispered to me, "Look!"

There they were, this war-torn people, waving an American flag in honor of what we had done for them. Those people, our new friends, were holding up our flag, a symbol of freedom, and now it symbolized theirs. There was not a dry eye on the Chinook as even the toughest soldiers shed a tear at the sight. It was an unforgettable moment forever engraved on the soles of our boots and our hearts.

We all face different combat zones in life. Whether it's the mental battles of doubt and depression or emotional and physical challenges of today's world. You need to look at the scuffs on your shoes, taking in what you've already overcome. Realize what you have done, but know there is still so much more to be stepped into and be discovered.

HERE IS A SUMMARY OF THE TIPS THAT HELPED ME WHEN HANDED UNEXPECTED SHOES:

★ Embrace the change in your plans and believe, this is what you are meant to do and where you are supposed to be.

★ List out the pros when handed unwelcomed events in your life. Choose to surround yourself with the positive, including people who build you up.

★ Never stop trying to learn more and step out of your comfort zone.

★ Fill your shoes in your own unique way.

★ Give of yourself. Get out and serve. When times are hard and the climb gets steep, make it about others. You will feel so much better when you take the focus off yourself. How can you markup someone else's soles for the better? Because when you do, it will also change your sole.

CHAPTER 4

You Expect Me to Wear These?

The shoes you never dreamed of wearing

"And the time came when the risk to remain
tight in a bud was more painful than the
risk it took to bloom."

ANAIS NIN

There are so many opportunities out there. It's fun to say "yes" to some, stepping out of your comfort zone, but you can't do them all. I was handed a new pair of shoes that made me laugh out loud when someone suggested I try them on, and I was okay to let this one pass by me. I am not one to pass up a new adventure when it lands in front of me, but this one seemed a little too farfetched to be *me*.

Someone approached me while on campus at SUU (Southern Utah University) and suggested I try on, not just any pair of shoes, but five-inch heels! They wanted me to try out for Miss SUU! When I first glanced at the shoes he was talking about, I thought they would make a good weapon. It took a lot of convincing to put them on, considering I was definitely stereotyping the other pageant girls with the same shoes. When I did give them a chance, I learned some pretty valuable lessons.

DON'T JUDGE A SHOE BY THE SIZE OF ITS HEEL

I had some preconceived notions of what I thought pageant girls were like from what I had heard and seen in the media. I have to be honest, when I was first approached by Del Beatty (Director of Student Involvement), I thought girls who wore those kinds of shoes were very self-serving. They looked like they just liked to wave their hand around, looking pretty.

How dare I judge that!

I was soon taught these girls can make a difference, create organizations, move people to action, and really change things for the better. I liked doing all those things, so I decided to give it a try. After breaking through my first lesson, I realized there was another anxiety holding me back before I fully committed to these shoes.

You think you are going to fail.

You're scared the end result won't work out as hoped. Maybe *scared* isn't the right word for it. Maybe we're mortified, embarrassed, or even disappointed in ourselves because our shoes are not turning out as expected. I knew there was a big chance I wasn't going to win, but why not just try and enjoy the growth in the process. Because, guess what? If you don't start on a path of growth because you have failed in the past and you're afraid, you are already *choosing to fail*. I'd much rather look back at my life and think, yeah I failed a few times, but at least I tried. At least I showed up and put myself out there, and in doing so, I learned some new things to help me become better. I choose to be proud of myself for trying.

Why not try again?

Each time you try, you will act slightly different, learning something new to help you in the future. If you are going about your goal the same way and getting the same result, you will continue to fail each time. It's up to you to change your plan of attack. Don't be scared to fail! Face your goal head on and you will grow, learn and become better than before. That is always a win!

Some people have the misconception that they can only do something once they *know everything* about it first. This is another one of the many anxieties we face as we set down new trails. The problem is the risk of loosing interest and vision of why you were even researching it in the first place, as well as losing sight of the end goal. The important thing to remember is to commit and learn as you go.

Some research is good, and needed beforehand, but sometimes people get so stuck in the learning phase they never actually start. Eventually, something else ends up pulling them away and they have no scuffs to show on their shoes. They never stepped into the adventure where most of the learning takes place.

You need to ask yourself, "What is the next step I need to take?" That's all you need to know. By putting one foot in front of the other, you will be taking yourself just a little bit further than you were before.

The smallest step makes the biggest difference.

I had so much to learn in this pageant combat zone (that's what it felt like to me at times), so I just took it one step at a time.

Sign up.

Take the plunge.

Learn as you go.

I loved how Rachel Hollis called it the "3 C's". Make the Choice, Commit, then stay Consistent in learning all you can. That's the best way to learn- while you are in the thick of it. What does that look like?

I showed up to all the workshops, months before the competition, learning how to put on make-up instead of camouflage paint and walk in high heels instead of combat boots. After a few months, I started to discover this woman inside of me I never knew was there, and surprisingly, I loved her! There was a part of me that didn't know how to be "girly," and trying on these new pairs of shoes helped me discover that side. I never would have uncovered these talents or skills had I not had the courage to try on these new pair of shoes and just go for it! Then, and only then, did I learn so much along the way.

When they announced me as the new Miss SUU, I couldn't believe it! I guess I missed the workshop on how you're supposed to respond when you win a pageant. I lost all my poise, as I started cheering and pumping my fist up and down like I was at a basketball game. After my unladylike outburst, the pageant director pulled me aside to advise me on my reaction for next time. I sputtered at this. *Next time?* I didn't realize it at the time, but my new race was just beginning—in five-inch heels.

Sometimes, new shoes land in front of us and new dreams come our way, taking us on a journey of discovery. *Miss Utah?* I couldn't believe my life had taken me to this point, now competing on the stage for Miss America! Definitely don't judge a shoe before trying it on.

BEING TRUE TO *YOU* AND STANDING UP FOR WHAT YOU BELIEVE NO MATTER WHAT

I was taught from a young age to dress modestly, and even though it's not for everyone, it was important to me. I made a decision from the beginning of my pageant competitions to wear modest clothes that weren't too revealing. Other contestants chose to show their own style, and though I chose mine, and we were still all friends. It didn't matter what our personal goals were—we still supported each other in our differences.

All the contestants were flown to Los Angeles to be part of a reality show, to showcase the changes they were making to the Miss America Organization. They were trying to become more "modern." Each day, we had friendly competitions, make-overs, and tips to help us for the final Miss America event. Since there was a high priority to make the show great, top fashion designers were brought in to play a part in running some of the competitions for the reality show. Each day brought new games and challenges from new designers. During the week, in the midst of all the excitement, as a surprise, one of the designers was going to randomly select one of us for a one-on-one session, and before I knew it, he was selecting me!

I got so nervous and thought to myself, *Oh no, how do I do this tactfully and not offend this special guest?* My concern was that the only gowns he had brought were all sleeveless. Luckily, the cameras paused as a plane flew by, causing too much noise, so I had more time to think the situation through, or just panic more. I said a quick prayer and asked for guidance (and hopefully have more planes fly by).

As the camera's started rolling again, the designer started his exciting announcement of choosing one contestant. My heart started pounding nervously as he then calls out, "Miss Louisiana!" My jaw just dropped and I caught my breath. *How did that happen? Ha! My prayers were answered!* I didn't have to go through with it.

While I was off with the rest of the contestants, getting tips from his team, I wasn't paying too much attention because it was all about showing more skin. Then out of the blue, Jenny, Miss New Mexico, comes up to me in tears. My first thought was how I could help. I couldn't help my medic instincts coming out.

It turns out, while the cameras were paused, waiting for the plane to fly by, word got out that I was the one that was selected. Jenny pulled the host aside, telling him how Miss Utah only wears gowns with sleeves. She asked if the guest fashion consultant had any, which they didn't. So, they let the guest know to call up another girl. Jenny felt like she now owed me an apology, feeling bad she spoke for me. She was worried she might have messed up my opportunity to work with a top fashion guru, and she started to cry, which triggered me to cry, too. I told her how grateful I was to her that she did that for me. She was an answer to my prayers, and my tears were of gratitude. I will never forget what Miss New Mexico did for me.

Throughout the years of competing in pageants, I made that decision from the beginning to let my true self shine out, no matter how different it was from everyone else. I was still me until the very end, doing push-ups on live television with my five-inch heels, surrounded by other Miss America finalists!

"Do what you feel in your heart to be right - for you'll be criticized anyway."

ELEANOR ROOSEVELT

Don't give into pressure around you if it is pulling you away from who you are and what you believe in. Your value and worth is way more important than going along with everyone else just to fit in.

LOVING WHO YOU ARE AND LETTING YOUR DIFFERENCES SHINE

The difficult part of pageants wasn't necessarily in all the preparation, but instead the aftermath of being crowned the winner.

The judges had pages of comments about what they thought of me. I had just won, so I figured I would be reading comments about all the things they liked about me, giving me a good boost after my hard work. I couldn't have been more wrong! It turns out most of the judges didn't seem to like me at all. After reading over the pages of comments, I wondered how I had even won!

There was paragraph after paragraph of them putting me down. I was hurt. I understood everyone is entitled to their opinion, but it was horrible when they started commenting on my character and who I was.

The judges picked at every little detail, whether it was me being in the army or my overall personality. It was like they couldn't believe someone could do both.

Reading the comments didn't give me the pick-me-up I was hoping for. Their words were tearing me up inside. Comments like that, whether from a pageant show or our own personal social media accounts, can do that to us. Many comments can be positive, giving you encouragement, but the occasional negative comment can slip in, becoming your focus and leaving your positive comments in the dust. Just one can tear your worth apart, causing you to lose the courage to go after your dreams.

After a few days of reading and focusing so much on those judges' comments, I wondered if this was really the direction for me. Maybe, I didn't really want it anymore. I was getting tired of the pageant life and was anxious to get on with something new. After a while though, I remember thinking, *why am I allowing this to hurt me? I know I can't please everyone. I can't make everyone happy. I'm not pizza!*

I didn't want to give up. This felt right, and I needed to stay focused on my target and keep moving forward. Though the mental battles still waged as I frantically tried to prepare myself, I stayed strong in reminding myself of the end goal.

Roughly a week before the Miss America competition, I was still an emotional wreck thinking about what was truly about to take place. *I'm competing for Miss America? What was I thinking? Can someone please send me back to a foxhole in Afghanistan, where I can just be in my camo saving lives?*

I have met all of these amazing women through the reality show and other events. Now, I was supposed to compete with them, hoping they'd mess up? I started to think about all the talented women, then started to compare myself to their looks and accomplishments.

Miss Georgia has such beautiful hair. Maybe, I should have cut mine like that.

Miss Indiana models so gracefully. All I have is a soldier strut.

Miss California sings like an angel. I shouldn't have picked singing for my talent. There is no way I will sound as good as her.

On and on I went with these thoughts in my head. It was a downward trap to get stuck into. Comparing myself to others is almost too natural, as if its second nature. It's scary to think of it being so common for us that most of the time we aren't even aware we're doing it, like breathing! Yet, comparing doesn't add to our life like taking a breathe does. It tears us apart from the inside out mentally, emotionally, and even physically.

While I was in this comparison pit of despair, one of our neighbors must have noticed the state I was in, deciding to drop by for a visit. In her hands was a book called *I Like Myself* by Karen Beaumont. She explained what this book had done for her growing up and even for her kids now.

She and her kids recite their favorite line each day:

"I like myself. I'm glad I'm being me. There is no one else I'd rather be." (I Like Myself, pgs. 1-2)

After she left, my mom and I read through the rest of the book. We both got emotional at the simple, yet powerful message the book delivered. We started talking and had the same idea: every contestant needed to hear this! Especially during one of the hardest weeks most of these girls have probably ever faced. We wondered how we could get this done in such a short amount of time. I was leaving in four days, and the competition started in one week. This was before mainstream social media.

I quickly found out, when you start talking to neighbors, word of mouth spreads fast. By the next day, friends and local teachers from the elementary school wanted to help out. We ordered fifty-one hardcover books of *I Like Myself*, and they arrived the day before I left.

My mom and I couldn't believe this was all coming together so quickly. My mom got some ribbon to tie around each book, and she helped me write a message we printed out on stickers to place on the cover of each book for the contestants. This is the message I wanted each girl to know:

You are beautiful, both inside and out! I am so privileged to have been able to have my path cross with yours over these past few months. We live in a world of harsh judgments. We are judged by our behavior, by our looks, by our clothes, by our actions, by our words. Never let those judgments diminish the incredible value that comes from the inside—the value of knowing you are, a daughter of God.

> *This is your week to shine, my friend…*
> *"'Cause nothing in this world you know*
> *can change what's deep inside, and so…*
> *No matter if they stop and stare,*
> *no person ever, anywhere*
> *can make me feel that what they see*
> *is all there really is to me." (I Like Myself, pgs. 19-21)*

All my love,
Miss Utah

I truly wanted each and every contestant to believe that! After all the books were ready, I went to the housekeeping staff of the Planet Hollywood Resort in Las Vegas, where Miss America was for just a few years before heading back to its original home in New Jersey. I had the staff place a book on the pillow of every contestant, so when they arrived, they would be able to read it before the big competition.

Now, I felt ready.

Even if I had a soldier strut, I was going to strut all over that stage and show them *me*. This was my voice, and I was going to belt it out loud. This was my style, and I needed to show them who I was. I loved who I was and still do!

I felt the biggest weight off my shoulders. Just like this "comparison brick" was weighing me down, holding me back from being my true self. Comparison is like a disease meant to cripple you. We don't know what loads other's carry or what circumstances they are in. Comparisons are not fair to us or others. Your biggest challenge in life isn't someone else. The only thing that matters is comparing the old with the new within YOU.

Take care of yourself to the point where you're able to look in the mirror and love yourself, then make the rest of the day about helping others.

We all certainly can do better.

We are all meant to shine.

YOU DIDN'T GET THE JOB, BUT YOU STILL NEED TO BELIEVE

I didn't win Miss America, so my life sucked and I was just going to be flipping burgers the rest of my life, scrubbing floors with a toothbrush. *That was not happening!* Maybe you didn't get the position or job you were working so hard for, but you keep working for it. Your time will come, and another door will open by trying on new shoes. You are meant for something far better, so see where your feet will take you!

You will be surprised by some shoes that will land in front of you throughout your life.

SOME TIPS THAT HELPED ME TO STAY ON TRACK WITH NEW ADVENTURES:

★ Don't judge the adventure before trying it out. See where it leads, and how far those shoes can take you. It's exciting to think about the possibilities and what you'll unravel about yourself in the process.

★ Follow authentic people and only get on social media when you need inspiration. It will help you stay on track. Never get on Social Media just to browse and fill up down time. You will just feel like you are not measuring up. Get on when we need an idea for a workout or words of inspiration to keep at it. Ever since I started these new tactics, it helped me run through those combat zones of comparisons and stay on track.

★ As you branch out, be sure to stay true to yourself and what you believe in. You will change and grow, wearing different shoes, but there's a part of you that carries through to every aspect of your life. Stand up for what you believe, and remind yourself of the reasons you get up every day. No one can change that about you.

★ Remember, throughout all your shoes, to love the uniqueness you bring to them. Love yourself in the process of growing.

CHAPTER 5

"I Got This. Wait, What Was I Thinking?"

The shoes you dreamt of wearing, but they didn't turn out as you envisioned

---

"People lose their way when they lose their why."

MICHAEL HYATT

You have been dreaming of the chance to wear these shoes your whole life. Whether it's finally landing your dream job, working toward a new hobby, or learning a new skill. *You've done it!* But you put them on, and things aren't going as smoothly as you hoped.

It's much harder than you imagined. Maybe the skill is harder, maybe the people you're working with are difficult.

For me, I dreamed of becoming a nurse—a mother for even longer—and prepared most of my life to acquire the necessary skills. Of course, I went to college then nursing school, graduating top of my class, but it didn't seem to help when I first put on my nursing shoes.

I had also been taking notes on motherhood most of my life as well, often meeting other mothers that emulated the type I wanted to be. I felt overly prepared, that I was ready for anything! (I am laughing to myself as I write this about my naive self before becoming a mother).

I felt confident!

HUMILITY. SOMETIMES, YOU HAVE TO LET OTHERS CARRY YOU

After a long road, with a few different shoes that were fun to try on, my dream of being a nurse was finally becoming a reality. As a new graduate, stepping into an Emergency Room for my first job was quite overwhelming. This was it! No more robot mannequins, classrooms, or shadowing another nurse to always fall back on. I walked into a room, I was *the* nurse, and they were my patients.

I put on my nursing shoes.

Even though I had learned so much in classes and from my other experiences, I still had so much to learn and discover in these shoes.

Sometimes, it's good to look back on your accomplishments so far, as you put on new shoes, facing new challenges. The life of a nurse can be quite stressful, as unique situations are thrown at you, especially in a critical care setting like the Emergency Department. I have put myself through stressful situations already.

I could handle this, *right?*

Part of me was so excited to finally be stepping into my dream as a Critical Care Nurse, but I couldn't hide the fact that deep down I was tachycardic, tachypneic, diaphoretic, and nauseous. Sounds like *I* needed the nurse.

The big anxiety we all face: *concerned you are the only one that feels this way and if you ask for help people will find out "your secret".*

I felt like I was the only one that felt this way. I was nervous about my job and shouldn't ask for help because I should know it all by now, right? Wrong. Stepping into your new shoes is where the real education begins. My managers and other staff became *my nurse* in a way.

When I needed help, other nurses were there to guide me. I had managers to help me stay focused and on the right track. I hate to admit it, but it took me a couple years to finally feel confident at my job, where I didn't have to ask for help as much. It's okay to be confident, but never stop asking questions. Find others in your field, or shoes, that have been doing it longer. Talk to them and keep learning. There is no shame in that. Asking shows you are eager to grow. Then, as you gain more experience, your strengths will help others at times too.

I chose pediatrics because of how I fell in love with the kids in Afghanistan. I love their honesty and how they keep playing no matter what.

There were shifts that took everything from me, though. I often wondered if I could do it again. Seeing children so close to death, hanging on for life while we attempted everything possible for them, was sometimes more than I could handle. Some kids made it, and some didn't. Though I had my moments, I tried to be as strong as possible. I've caught numerous nurses from falling because they couldn't handle another death, but they've also done the same for me. We would carry each other out, hearts breaking and knees weak, leaning on one another as we cried, when some patients took a turn for the worse.

We were in this *together*.

I have gotten angry at God sometimes, wondering why he would let this child go. Even though I didn't really know them, I still loved them and wanted them to live. Why did this have to happen? Why did this child have to die? Then during a shift on a long night, I gained a new perspective. I was one of the nurses maintaining care while the rest of the team handled a critical care patient. Yes, I loved this child. I loved them for just existing and being who they are, but God loves *and knows* this child unlike anyone else. His love is so much deeper. How much harder on Him must this be as He sees all of us go through these humbling challenges, bringing us to our knees? Yet, He is there listening to our cries. He is there to catch us in our fall or to push us up our mountain, no matter the shoes we're in. You might think you are the strong one in a situation, then, out of the blue, you realize you can't do it on your own.

We all fall at different times and it can take us by surprise. We can't do it alone all the time, and God is not only there to carry us at times, but help fill our shoes the rest of the way. He gives us these experiences so we don't forget Him and lets us know He is there to help, whether our plan or prayer didn't get answered in the way we expected. Whether our burden is lighter or completely goes away, it is by God that all things are possible. There have been many days as a nurse, a mother, a soldier, and a runner even, that I have seen and felt God's hand in my life. No matter the shoe I'm wearing, God is always there (looking back, I can see that, but in the moment may not have always seen it), helping me fill my shoes with what I couldn't do on my own. God has been there for you and will be there for you no matter the scuffs and mistakes you have made. He will help you reach a whole new potential you never thought possible.

KEEPING PERSPECTIVE

I always considered myself an optimistic person, until I had kids. Now, I feel like I am the biggest complainer! I whined and complained about everything. Okay, sometimes I *still* whine and complain, especially as my life gets more and more out of control with each kid coming along, and I still don't know what I am doing. I thought I would have had this figured out by now.

Working in the Emergency Department gave me a lot of perspective. I met some incredible kids and also some amazing parents who took care of them. I was honored to be their nurse as I saw the optimistic attitude and resilience they had. Some of these families would live at the hospital for weeks, even months, while their children not only had surgery after surgery, but multiple illnesses topped with more diagnosis and problems. Yet, they took every challenge with a positive attitude. Going to work at times was like a school for building my character. It caused some deep reflections and helped me to never take my life and comforts for granted.

When I am mopping the floor for the fourth time and it's barely breakfast time, I reflect. I have one child crying about I don't even know what, another is telling me every detail of their dream, the baby is emptying out yet another cupboard, and I step on an action figure, which is an eight on the pain scale of 0-10, as I run to prevent another catastrophe between my other kid and the fireplace. I stop myself and try to gain perspective.

I try to start listing things I'm grateful for instead. It's a tactic you have probably heard over and over before, and by now it's lost its "Ah-ha!" factor, but it works! It has helped me stop complaining almost instantly!

How lucky am I to have four healthy kids that leave crumbs all over the floor? How cute are they when they bring in muddy footprints because they were being creative outside? I'm thankful my body is healthy enough to clean up after them. How lucky am I to have a home and yard for my kids to safely play around?

So many times we compare ourselves and envy those who have it better. We think our life just isn't good enough because we don't have *this* or *that*, but you must realize that blessings already surround you. One of my favorite sayings I have had my kids memorize is, "It is not happy people who are grateful. It is grateful people who are happy." There is strength in gratitude, and seeing your blessings in the little things will empower you get through the day-to-day grind.

I get that there are also circumstances we are handed in life that knock us off our feet—whether good or bad. For example, let's add a new little soul to your family. This is an amazing circumstance, but it also comes with a lot of sleepless nights, hospital bills, and major adjustments in life. Moving. Changing jobs. An illness or diagnosis changing your course. These can all be viewed as good and bad situations.

We know we cannot always change our circumstances, but our thoughts about them are something we do have control over. After an event happens in life, it is our thoughts that make it good or bad.

Let that sink in for a moment. Your thoughts about a situation are creating negative or positive feelings. It's important to recognize which one it is because you have the choice to accept or deny your thoughts, and the power they have over you.

I've witnessed this process time and time again, when family's lives were completely changed by a cancer diagnosis for their little girl, or their son develops diabetes. They now have to learn how to manage the new pair of shoes they were just handed. They couldn't change the diagnosis and say, "Sorry, we don't like that one, can we get another diagnosis, please?" They couldn't change their circumstances, but they did have control on how they felt about it.

Some were so bitter it affected everyone they came in contact with. It affected their feelings which then spilled over into their everyday actions. Others were scared, but knew this was happening no matter what, so they made the best out of the situation. It was hard, and I was humbled every time I got to work with families like this, but they put on those shoes, plowing new trails, picking others up along the way, encouraging them.

EMBRACING FAILURE

As I started out in my motherhood shoes, I wondered how I was going to fill them especially because, let's face it, there really isn't any one single pair of shoes that fits motherhood. It seems that each step down this trail requires a change in footwear to help me successfully traverse this adventure. The terrain is ever changing!

All of a sudden you become the CEO of your household while earning your PhD in everything your kid needs: a chef to picky eaters, a taxi driver, a teacher, a soother, a mediator—and the list can go on while most have full-time jobs of their own.

Considering what we do as mothers and me just starting that path, I wondered what type of mom I would be. Would I be the fun mom? Would I be the kind of mom that made them eat their vegetables before leaving the table? Would I be a soccer mom, shuffling them and their friends to games? No matter what, I knew I had the opportunity to make anything happen I wanted to.

We all have that opportunity to decide who we are and what we are made of, even if our shoes are worn out and we aren't proud of some of the stories. You have the power to *change* your course and step up to a whole new *you*.

Even though I visualized the type of mom I would be… almost a decade into it now, I am not that person exactly.

There are things I'm proud of and feel I know how to take on well. Yet there are also traits that have surprised me that I am honestly disappointed in myself for becoming. I didn't know I would become such a reactive mom who loses control and yells way more often than I would like to admit. I typically love things to be in order (as I am sure most do) but if you look at my house now, I guess you can say have my messes in order. I get to the clutter piles each week but like I heard from another mom once, keeping a house clean with kids is like brushing your teeth while eating oreos.

Even though my scuffs on these shoes didn't quite turn out like I had dreamt doesn't mean that it's permanent. I have my good days and bad days but I never want to stop trying, getting closer to that person I envisioned when I first put on these shoes.

Don't linger on the scuffs you're ashamed of; you are more than that. Be proud of your marks as you change the pace and direction you are now heading with your shoes.

Not all of you reading this are nurses or mothers, but we all wear shoes at some point that seem like an ordinary part of life, but may be our toughest shoes yet. Others might be going through the same thing, making it look easy. So easy, in fact, it makes you throw out some choice words just out of frustration! Deep down, they're probably struggling just as much as you are. We feel like we are swimming upstream in rapids without a lifejacket, while others are floating on a comfy raft with an umbrella and an ice-cold drink.

Every person fills their shoes differently.

We all walk our own path and can't wear the shoes of someone else. As I mentioned before, don't judge a shoe by the size of its heel before trying it on, and don't judge the scuffs on others' shoes. We don't know what someone has been through, and while we know we—literally and figuratively—can't walk a mile in someone else's shoes, we can be more understanding of what their stories might tell.

We can help each other, lift each other up, and push each other along instead of sticking out a foot so they trip. I keep tripping just like everyone else. There are days I look back, ashamed of how dealt with a situation, and I sometimes wonder if I'm meant to wear these shoes. Are they the right fit? I needed and still need help.

Something that's helped me when I feel like I don't know what I'm doing is to look to others who are running this same journey. There are other people's stories which, at times, help push us along or may even carry us. I still slip and stumble, but the fall isn't as hard, and I have friends right there to catch and guide me.

The topic of failure when going after new things and setting bigger goals is important, but what if you're already living your dream; living it and failing?

Struggling at times, that's normal. It's something we all face. Sometimes you go through the same lessons over and over. Don't let that get you down! The way I see it is if I fail again, I want to make sure I fail *better*.

"I have been bent and broken, but - I hope - into a better shape."
Emily Dickinson

DON'T WEAR OUT YOUR "SOLE"

After a few years of trying to do it all, wearing all these different shoes, especially now as a mother of four, I felt like I was losing my spark. I was losing a piece of myself. I was getting burned out easily, I wanted to cry every time my kids whined or fought, and I felt like I was about to explode as I was running through this new minefield, trying to handle it all.

Just like my experience running through a minefield when first arriving in Afghanistan, mines can be very ordinary, everyday things. They're enticing, but dangerous.

Our lives are full of mines. They are planted everywhere and disguised as ordinary, everyday life among circumstances or people we come across. You could be at work and your boss adds another project to your lap to be done in a short amount of time. You tackle the dishes and somehow throw a decent meal together for dinner, while five loads of laundry are still piled on the couch needing to be folded and every bathroom has been neglected. The messes at work or home may pile up to distract or deter us from reaching our potential. Sometimes I feel like I have to triage, or assign degrees of urgency, with the surprises that come my way.

Some items in my mind get the "red tag" for things I need to address immediately in my work or home life. Others get the delayed with a "yellow or green tag," knowing I can get to the matter a little later. Then, there are those items that are just hopeless, maybe some room in my house, and I just close the door. Those get the "black tag."

When you feel like you're running through minefields of your own, don't let those distractions take you off your path.

Get to what you can. Triage the things in your life needing your attention the most at the moment.

I understood, after a while, that each of my challenges have only made me stronger because I've learned, making the best of them. *What's the use though if I don't put into practice what I've learned?* I then realized the information I was sharing with others were things I needed for myself more than ever. I was so focused on my kids, and the never-ending to-do lists, that I was running out of fuel. I still needed to take care of myself.

On this journey of discovering what your next pair of shoes is going to be, it's important you don't neglect *you*. You can get caught up in the *to-do* list of the everyday, and your overall goals, but if you are not taking care of yourself, it can really hurt you in the long run. Take it one step at a time, making sure you're taking care of yourself along the way.

Here are some things I've touched on throughout the book that I've learned and have helped me when the climb got too steep:

Become more of a morning person.

I have lived and learned the value of this tool most of my life. I know the benefits of getting a head start in the morning. You are more on your game, ready to show up better for everything else during the day. If you try to cram in those things to take care of you at the end of the day, it just won't be as effective. I've fallen into the rut a couple of times, finding I was really cutting those things short that were so valuable to build me up.

Now, it doesn't have to be 4:30 a.m., but if you get up just thirty minutes earlier than usual every morning, you might be shocked by how good you feel. Remember, one step at a time, and you will be surprised with how much more you can tackle.

<u>Visualize yourself in the shoes:</u>

Picture every detail of you accomplishing your goal. This is a little different than a vision board. I visualize me in that day I am about to start. I am more present. It is not about picturing my goals over the next ten years, but more of, how do I want to show up today? I do this with little goals, like not yelling at my kids after a rough day I'm not proud of. I want to make sure those kinds of days are happening less and less. I picture myself being the mom I want to be. I see myself joking and laughing with my kids. I see myself letting things go easier, not being so reactive. Before I head into a shift in the hospital, I picture myself handling the busy schedule. I run through different scenarios to help me get in the right mindset.

Visualizing has helped me be more *on target* with my day-to-day self. Seeing myself *being* the person I want to be each day means I am *her* more often.

<u>Affirmations:</u>

There is power in talking positively to yourself out loud! Start with saying even just three things you like about yourself in the mirror. It's weird at first, but it makes such a difference. Then, add three qualities you want to acquire or goals you have. Say them out loud! Here are just a few examples of ones I have said but they are constantly changing and reshaping:

- I'm a good mom because…and I list out the reasons why.
- I'm a runner. I'm taking care of myself, and my body is stronger. I will run this pace by xx/xx date and will sign up for this race.
- I'm a good nurse because I care about doing my best. I continue learning new things to help in patient care. I put the patient first.
- I'm devoted to my husband and family. They are the most important people in my life. I will show signs of love every day to each of them.

Affirmations can be powerful!

I have even started to recite a few affirmations with my kids on occasion to help them plant the seed in their brains now, so it's more familiar to them as they grow. Here are some examples I changed for my kids:

- I'm a son/daughter of God, and I am loved no matter what.
- I'm in control of my emotions.
- I'm okay if I don't get my way. My life is special because of me.
- I'm important, and I have a purpose.

Okay, so some might call it brainwash instead of affirmations with my kids but why not fill their heads with positive thinking about themselves.

The most important idea is that it's okay to tell yourself how awesome you are! Whether you can think of three affirmations or even just one, the crucial part is that you start somewhere.

Eating healthy and exercise:

We have heard this all of our lives about what eating healthy and exercising does for you. It helps you be your best self so you can tackle your dreams. Eat and do things that bless your body, not tear it apart and break it down.

Reading:

This one has been the hardest for me because I never seem to find a book that grabs me—until this last year. I set a goal to read a new book each month, and not just any books, but books that inspire me to be better. Reading from authors that emulate how I want to be, and have tools for me to learn has made such an impact on my life.

I have been more motivated by making sure I include all of these steps each day. Even if it's just one page of reading or a few minutes on each area, it makes a difference. Most of these tools I've mastered and performed for the last couple decades, but I've only recently added the reading. It takes some extra focus and scheduling on my part to make sure I do read each day but when I factor in all of these tools, it gives me an even better edge to my day and life.

Self-care will never hurt you. It will help you strive to be your best self. *Why only be at your best part of the time?* We have all made those excuses. I'm talking about those days off, weekends, vacations, or busy periods in our life that we validate ourselves by slacking off. I was guilty of all of these until I woke up and asked, "*Why* am I doing this to myself?"

When the weekend, or a vacation, would come around I used to get so excited because I could slack off my diet and goals. I could hang around the house without a care in the world, but when Monday trudged along, it made it that much harder to get back to *my life*.

I hated that feeling.

So, I decided to change the concept, keeping more to my routine as much as possible on vacations and during free time. I still indulged a little here and there, but I didn't completely throw everything out the window I had worked so hard to maintain. When I stay closer to my goals on my breaks, my life isn't thrown off course as much. Let's stop with the excuses of vacations, holidays, weekends, and being too tired from everyday life.

I'm always going to keep trying to put forth my best self always. Whatever shoe you are wearing, you have to take care of yourself...so you can be your *best* self.

You are not alone.

You have others running along with you who shine in their moments, and who will be there to help you. They also have their moments of slipping and stumbling, but you can be there to catch them as well.

We're in this race together! God is also alongside you, helping you fill your shoes as you face unbearable challenges you never imagined possible. Your shoes will get scuffed up, but on the other side of that mountain is a whole new you.

REMEMBER TO...

★ *Always be willing to ask for help.*

★ *List out your blessings*, especially during the more chaotic times. This method will help ground you.

★ *Push through the yucky muck*: Maybe you don't totally love what you are doing right now but you know it will get you to where you want to be. There are things many of us don't love about our dream jobs but we still do it. We still go through the grind, because we know we will be that much closer to obtaining our end goal. You have to be willing to do the grunt work when it comes to getting on the path that you are destined for.

★ *Prepare the night before for the next day.* Lay out those "shoes" or items you need to get your regular day to become a better day. You want to work out? Okay, lay out your clothes so they are ready for you to put on in the morning. Want to eat healthy? Prepare snacks and the right foods to have around and ready. Want to work on a new hobby? Have those shoes or necessary things laid out to tackle it.

★ *Take care of yourself*, so you can be at your best to care for others.

CHAPTER 6

Give Those Dreams of Yours Some Shoes

Go ahead and try on those new shoes

"What you get by achieving your goals is not as important as what you become by achieving your goals."

ZIG ZIGLER

Go look at the shoes you have in your closet. What are they telling you? What stories are they sharing? Maybe, you can only find one of the pairs and they are telling you to slip on some organizational shoes.

Out of all the shoes you have, which ones would you consider to be the most important ones? I can tell you the very pair. I am sure many of them hold some value, but there is only one that is the most essential.

It's the shoes you're wearing right now! It is in those shoes that you make the decision of what you are going to do next. Those shoes are who you are meant to be. What you are going to do about it?

This is it!

You have a new box of shoes to open. What are they? This is your time to shine. Step out of your comfort zone. Visualize your success to help drown out the doubt. Realize your thoughts are created by you, and practice gaining more positive control over them. Don't blend in when you were born to stand out. Have faith in the unknown, you were born to do this.

You are your biggest challenge, not anyone else.

CREATING YOUR LIFE PLAN

I have listed a few takeaways throughout the book, but there are certain ones that really fit into creating your life plan. These tips will help you stick with a plan for positive change. Let's put some of those main points together and show what this looks like:

Step 1: I picture myself in 10 years. I visualize the different shoes I *want* to be wearing, and what I am doing in them.

- Motherhood: I picture myself having a close relationship with each one of my kids. I picture my home organized and having structure.
- Wife: I see my husband and I loving each other more than ever.
- Nurse: I want to be a leader and motivating others.

- <u>Health/Fitness:</u> I want to continue to run. I want to have the energy and stamina to keep up with my kids, and remain healthy.
- <u>Fun hobbies:</u> I want to learn two new skills that have nothing to do with the above, but help keep life interesting and keep me learning.

Step 2: I ask myself- What do I need to do *now* to make sure that happens?

- <u>Motherhood:</u> Sit down with my kids and chat about their day or read a book, one on one. Have a night out with each of my kids individually, quarterly. Have them help in the planning of those nights. With areas that are disorganized in my home, I will list them out, triage them in the order that they need to be done and tackle those projects one at a time.
- <u>Wife:</u> Go on dates at least twice a month. Pick a project to work on together. Revisit our goals quarterly to keep our vision of ourselves and our family in tune with one another.
- <u>Nurse:</u> Volunteer for extra projects and roles, gaining experience and trust in the department. Work on becoming the Charge Nurse, Nurse Educator, then Nurse Manager.
- <u>Health/Fitness:</u> Give it my all for thirty minutes, five to six days a week, in exercising my body. Sign up for a race. Run a race with my kids to teach them the importance of exercise.
- <u>Fun hobbies:</u> Sign up for a class to learn my next skill and practice on a new project each month.

Step 3: Get out the monthly calendar: Be more intentional. Purposefully schedule in those goals you value. Everyone gets the same amount of time. It can control you or you can be in control of your time, making it matter. I schedule in those important dates with my husband and kids. I know when things I value are coming up; I make sure nothing conflicts with those events already scheduled.

This clear life plan will help you face, and may even prevent common anxieties that creep up and feel like rocks in our shoes. Let's recap our challenges along with the chapter for reference:

1) It's too hard (chapter 2)
2) Being uncomfortable (chapter 2)
3) Doubting your capabilities (chapter 2)
4) Fear of the unknown (chapter 3)
5) Needing to know everything first (chapter 4)
6) Comparison and measuring up (chapter 4)
7) Fear of failure (chapter 4)
8) I am alone in feeling like this and am embarrassed to ask for help (chapter 5)

The negative feelings will still come, but they won't be as strong or as often when you have this vision created of your life plan. The other lessons mentioned throughout the book will also feed that part of you to keep at it stronger. Don't forget, though, the lessons you have learned in your own shoes already have shaped you to maneuver through obstacles coming your way.

YOU ARE ENOUGH

Always know you are enough as you are. You are a person created so perfectly, and you were given unique gifts and talents to share. Never stop developing your talents. We are perfect by still progressing. Never stop learning and growing. If you don't develop your talents or continue to learn more—trying on new shoes—you can lose your skills, and reason for getting up every day.

"Our responsibility is to rise from mediocrity to competence, from failure to achievement. Our task is to become our best selves. One of God's greatest gifts to us is the joy of trying again, for no failure ever need to be final."

THOMAS S. MONSON
"THE WILL WITHIN", ENSIGN, MAY 1987, 68

You should never stay the same!

You either have purpose to grow or you diminish. So, always believe you are enough, and strive to improve. You are a vision of and *for* yourself. Going after a vision will only continue to develop who you uniquely are.

I never grew up thinking I would ever be wearing most of these shoes I've stepped into. We are so blessed to live in such a world that makes it possible to go after anything we can imagine. I still loved myself growing up, but also loved new opportunities that came my way, refusing to pass them up. Sometimes, new dreams land in front of you that you never thought were possible. Step into the unknown and go for it, because of the love you have for yourself. Don't ever do something because it has to complete you. Look back at what you have already done, but realize the many shoes you have yet to wear. They are tools to help you discover what's already there. Continue to discover yourself more on each journey, and seek what's deep inside you just waiting to be brought to light.

It's all you!

Friends, it's not always about the shoes really. It's about who you become and the stories you create while wearing them—the person you become in the process. Though you may never put on combat boots, five-inch heels, or run a marathon, there are so many shoes you can, and will, try on to tell your own story.

Just as the instruments and techniques we use in the Emergency Room were lifesaving interventions, these tools I have given you are vital to your life in order to get the most out of it. Don't sell yourself short.

You were made for more!

WHAT'S NEXT?

As for my life and what's next, I am *ALL IN*. I have a vision for my life. It's exciting to visualize the life I want, just like you can visualize the life you want, as well as what shoes we still have yet to wear. I'm crafting ideas all the time. Am I going to be the next CEO of a company or start another blog?

Who knows. Those aren't really goals of mine at this moment but life is always full of surprises. I am living my dreams right now, keeping my eyes open for more opportunities along the way. I will continue to speak to crowds and be there for a friend who needs a boost. I am an active participant in my life and love to sculpt it in a way that's unique to me.

Now, I know I am not in complete control of my life—working in the ER sure taught me that. Something could happen tomorrow. Our lives could change in an instant, but your vision can help you push through barriers, coming out on the other side as heroic as ever. When things change in an instant, I always refer to the catalogue of tools I have to navigate my life to get what I want. I'm fully aware something could come along and tackle me sideways, throwing me off course, but I hope to come out on top. I hope we all come out on top.

Acknowledgments

Many thanks to many people who were invaluable in the many shoes I have worn to always push me and keep me going.

To all my running partners that joined me in early morning runs and always signed up for the next "big one" with me.

To all the soldiers I served among in the 1/48 Infantry Division, "Bravo Bulldogs", 1/211 Aviation, 25th Infantry Division and MedCom who taught me so much about sacrifice and pushing yourself to new limits.

To Del Beatty, Lynne Smith, Renita Revill, and Sharlene Hawkes who helped me reach inside myself and discover new capabilities. Also to the Miss Utah Organization and the many contestants that made the hard journey fun and memorable.

To the staff at Primary Children's Emergency Dept. who continue to amaze me in their resiliency to care in the craziness and always put the child first. I grew every shift I worked with them.

To my dear friend and college roommate, Jessica Holinger for sharing her invaluable talents and time with me.

Amanda B. Photography for capturing moments that showcase the real "you".

To my amazing kids, Millie, Dani, Boston and Hudson who make each day an adventure and push me to keep trying. You are so patient with me and I am so glad we get to tackle each adventure together forever.

My mom and the gift she has been and is in my life. God knew I needed her, not just growing up but even now as I am all "grown up".

My husband for always being at my side and encouraging me with each new idea. I look forward to the many shoes I still have yet to wear and doing it all with you at my side.

About the Author

Between being a proud mom to four young kids and happily married housewife to Kerry, Jill Shepherd continues to inspire many as a professional speaker and author. She also remains a nurse in the emergency department at a Children's Hospital, bringing smiles to kid's faces. During her eight years in the US military service as a combat medic, she earned five medals for her outstanding service and the highest fitness award during Army Basic Training. She's a marathoner, former Miss Utah, sailor, and a "Woman of Strength" from one of four women chosen in *Muscle and Fitness Hers* Magazine. *Scuffed Up* is her debut book.

Reach out to Jill through:

Instagram: @jillkshep

Facebook: @jillkshep

Can You Help?

Thank You for Reading My Book!

I really appreciate all of your feedback, and I love hearing what you have to say.

I need your input to make the next version of this book and my future books better.

Please leave me an honest review on Amazon letting me know what you thought of the book.

Thanks so much!

Jill

CPSIA information can be obtained
at www.ICGtesting.com
Printed in the USA
LVHW040022100420
652901LV00002B/635

9 781734 363906